© 2013 Christian Art Gifts, RSA
Christian Art Gifts Inc., IL, USA

Designed by Christian Art Gifts

Images used under license from Shutterstock.com

Scripture quotations are taken from the *Holy Bible*,
New International Version® NIV®. Copyright © 1973, 1978, 1984
by International Bible Society. Used by permission of
Zondervan Publishing House. All rights reserved.

Scripture quotations are taken from the *Holy Bible*, New Living Translation®,
second edition. Copyright © 1996, 2004 by Tyndale House Publishers, Inc.,
Carol Stream, Illinois 60188.
All rights reserved.

Scripture quotations are taken from the
Contemporary English Version®.
Copyright © 1995 by American Bible Society.
All rights reserved.

Scripture quotations are taken from *The Message*.
Copyright © by Eugene H. Peterson, 1993, 1994, 1995,
1996, 2000, 2001, 2002 by NavPress Publishing Group.
Used by permission.

Printed in China

ISBN 978-1-4321-0620-1

Christian Art Gifts has made every effort to trace the ownership of all quotes
and poems in this book. In the event of any question that may arise from
the use of any quote or poem, we regret any error made and will be pleased
to make the necessary correction in future editions of this book.

© All rights reserved. No part of this book may be reproduced in any form
without permission in writing from the publisher, except in the case of brief
quotations embodied in critical articles or reviews.

13 14 15 16 17 18 19 20 21 22 – 10 9 8 7 6 5 4 3 2 1

Tweets for my Tweetheart

christian art gifts

#Love
makes every day *extra* special.

faith
hope
love

Love

is like a #beautiful_flower
which I may not touch,
but whose fragrance makes
the garden a place of delight.

@HelenKeller

Those who bring **#sunshine** into the lives of others cannot keep it from themselves.

@JamesM.Barrie

If we love one another, God lives in us and His love is made complete in us.

@1John4:12

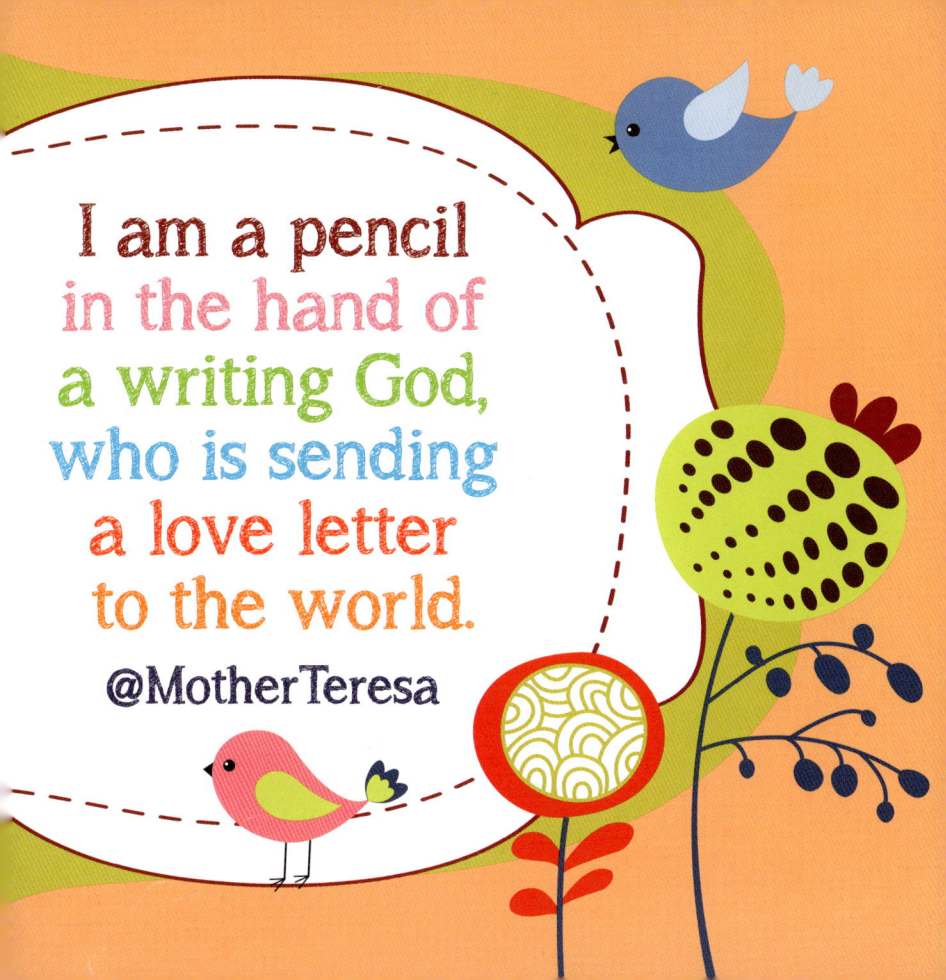

another

To #loveGod is the greatest of virtues; to be loved by God is the greatest of blessings.

Every good and perfect gift is from above, coming down from the Father of the heavenly lights. @James 1:17

The Lord your God
goes with you;
He will never leave you
nor forsake you.

@Deuteronomy31:6

for He is **good!**

His faithful **love** endures forever.

@Psalm 118:29

The sun can break through the darkest cloud; love can brighten the gloomiest day.

@ William Arthur Ward

so that everyone who believes in Him will not perish but have eternal life."
@John 3:16

If I had a flower for every time I thought of you ...

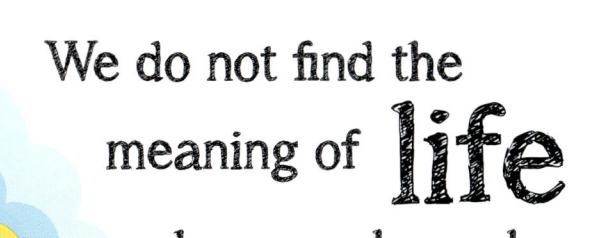

We do not find the meaning of life by ourselves alone – we find it with another.

@ThomasMerton

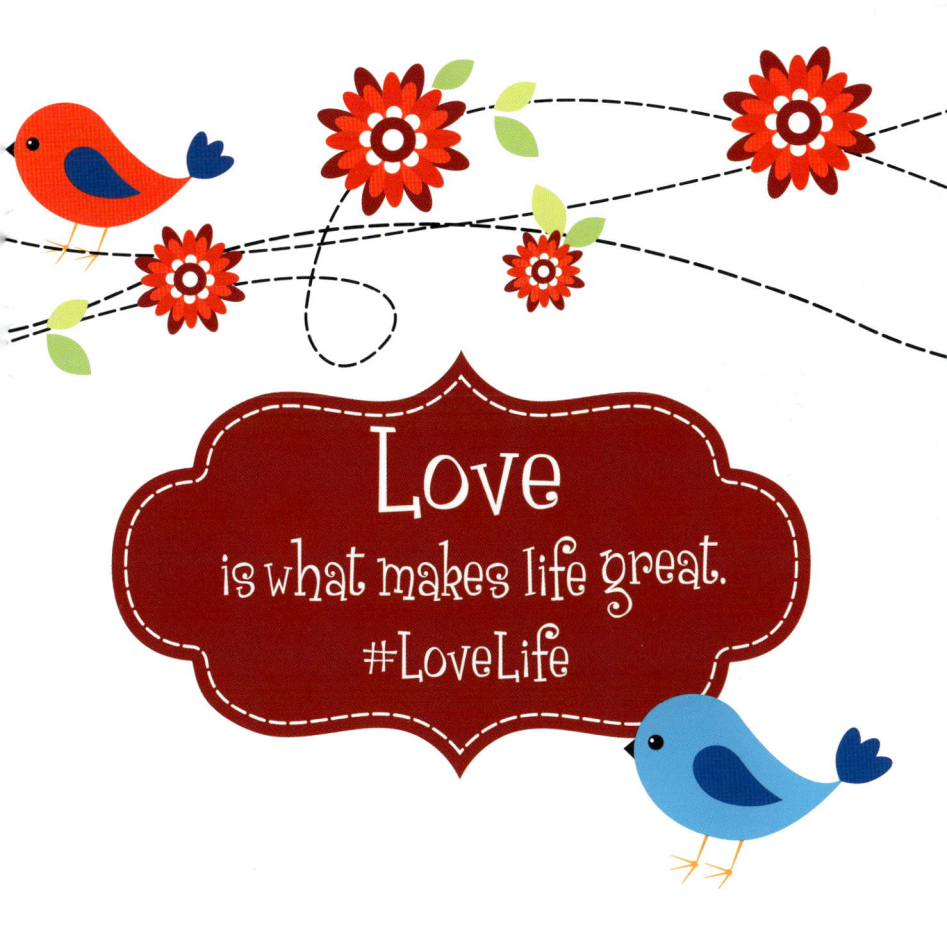

There is no surprise more magical than the surprise of being_loved. It is God's finger on man's shoulder.
@CharlesMorgan

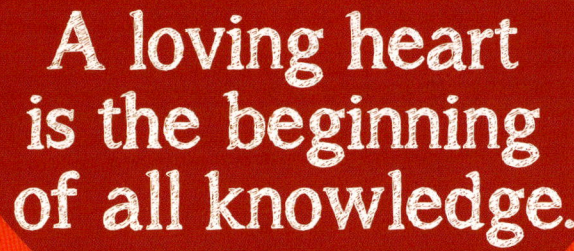

The Lord is good and His love endures forever; His faithfulness continues through all generations.

@Psalm 100:5

#Love accepts the trying things of life without asking for explanations. It trusts and is at rest. @AmyCarmichael

love

is the

energy of

Life.

@RobertBrowning

Whenever we are surrounded by friends who love us, we cannot help but #smile

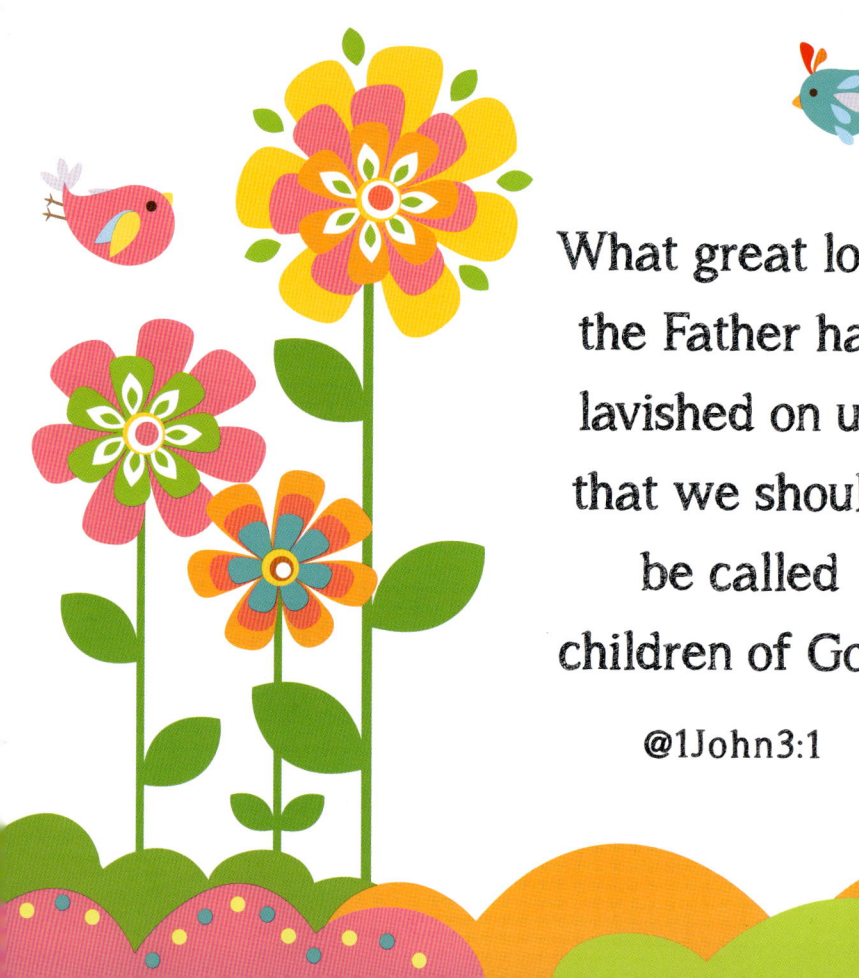